OBSERVATIONS
AT THE
BIRD FEEDER

60
DEVOTIONS

JANET LYNN PIERCE

Year of the Book
135 Glen Avenue
Glen Rock, PA 17327

ISBN: 978-1-64649-477-4 (paperback)
ISBN: 978-1-64649-478-1 (ebook)

Library of Congress Control Number: 2025902844

DEDICATION

I dedicate this book to my husband, who is always there, praying for me and encouraging me, in all my endeavors. To my sons, their wives and my grandchildren, may you always see the beauty God provides and know He walks with you to guide and protect you.

ACKNOWLEDGMENTS

First, thank you, God, for your patience, your provisions and for giving me the idea to see your wisdom in the antics of birds at the bird feeders. To my twin sister, Janyce Brawn, thank you for believing in me. Pauline Drozeski, you were the first to tell me I should put these writings into a book. You planted the seed, and the others in our Friday Nonfiction writers' group encouraged me to continue. To Dr. Rev. Steve Aguzzi for reading my book as one of the first beta readers, thank you. To the Sisterhood and other friends at my church, thank you for listening to my devotions as I continued to write through the seasons. To my other critique groups, Fellowship of the Quill (FOTQ) and Thursday Afternoon Critique (TAC), thank you for your encouragement.

To my editor and publisher Demi Stevens of Year of the Book, thank you for your guidance, advice and making this book a reality.

Observations at the Bird Feeder was a labor of love and learning as I witnessed birds at my feeders and delved into Scriptures to support the way I viewed the actions to explain my thoughts. I pray everyone who reads this book is blessed.

Follow my blog www.janetpierceswritingcafe.com

I would love to hear from you. Email: jlpierce494@gmail.com

CONTENTS

God's Provision

Glossary

INTRODUCTION

If someone had told me ten years ago, I would be writing about what I could see out my greatroom window as I ate breakfast, I would have thought they were crazy. But that's exactly what I've been doing, observing.

It started with a red bird feeder I stuck in the ground right outside my window. I could sit at the dining room table and look out into my backyard and the woods. One Mother's Day, my younger son gave me a second bird feeder that he attached to the railing on my porch. It had a camera so that I could watch the birds up close on my phone. Now, as I sit and listen to my Bible app on my phone while eating breakfast, I watch the visitors to the two feeders. With a county park around two-thirds of my back yard, we get a lot of birds.

In retirement, with more time to contemplate as I listened to Scripture each morning, I began to wonder about the western Pennsylvanian avian visitors at my bird feeders. For each new bird I observed, I looked up information online to help me relate to what I saw and what I wrote. I have compiled a glossary of these birds as well as some websites readers can visit for more information.

My time watching my avian visitors led me to write the devotions within this book. It is organized by themes and shows a progression of how we might pray: giving thanks, waiting upon the Lord, putting him first, knowing God is there with us and loves us, how as we wait, we should seek God's will and realize the ways in which He provides for us. You may choose to read it by topic or chapter, once a week since there are over 52, or however you wish. If you read one a week you might decide to read it on day one of that week, then each day see how the observation applies to your life or how you can use it in the future. In each devotion, I have tried to capture what I learned about the birds, myself, and my walk with God. I hope and pray these observations may help you know and understand that a God who has created a world full of majesty and wonder, who cares for the birds of the air, also cares for you.

BEING THANKFUL

Long Time No-See Nuthatch

The birds are enjoying a hearty breakfast today. Black-capped chickadees vie with tufted titmice and house finches for food. Suddenly a white-breasted nuthatch glides onto the pole, then the bird feeder. I suck in my breath and grab my camera.

I haven't seen one of these white-breasted nuthatches in ages. I smile and snap a few shots of the bird. My feeling of happiness when it appears is similar to what I feel when I greet family members. It is so relaxing and comforting to spend time with people I haven't seen in months.

The bird's vivid black, white, and gray plumage stands out as it arches its head to get food. It is obviously a male since the female of that species is duller in color. The scene makes me wonder. How often do we stop to thank God for the simple things in life: for the beauty of the outdoors, for the birdsong that surrounds us, and for our family? Not often enough, I think.

As the Bible says in Colossians 4:2, "Devote yourselves to prayer, being watchful and thankful." So, the next time I see a bird or my family, I'll give thanks to God for all he has wondrously made.

Prayer: Dear God, your creation is astounding. Open my eyes, my heart and my soul to be aware and to give thanks for your bounty and blessings that surround me. Amen.

Figure 1: Long Time No-See Nuthatch

Grooming

I am just sitting down to eat breakfast when I notice a tufted titmouse grooming itself, first on the top of my windchimes next to the bird feeder and then on top of the crook of the feeder. Birds groom? It is either grooming its feathers or pecking at its feet. Then I ask myself whether it has food in its beak that needs to be broken into smaller pieces. The idea of a bird grooming itself reminds me of how I wash my face, brush my hair and put on makeup – my grooming for the day.

As I sit here watching the birds I realize my meditation, reading and listening to the Bible, and praying for family and friends is another way of grooming—a heavenly, spiritual grooming for the day ahead. I'm so glad I have the time and solitude to do this in the morning. How do you groom yourself for the day?

Prayer: Dear God, thank you for time, solitude, and the ability to watch the birds, your messengers that prompt me to listen to your Word and the Holy Spirit as I groom myself for the day ahead. In Jesus' name I pray, Amen.

The Unwanted Guest

A chipmunk has been coming to eat the seeds below my bird feeder for quite a while now. His name is Alvin because he is just as fearless and persistent as Alvin in the old television cartoon "Alvin and the Chipmunks." Not knowing his gender, I call him a "he." I post a picture on Facebook of him gorging on the seeds below the bird feeder. Those seeds are for the mourning doves, cardinals, and other birds who prefer to eat on the ground.

A friend calls Alvin the "unwanted guest" which makes me think of two stories from the Bible. The first one, in Luke 16:19-21, talks about Lazarus, the poor man who wants to eat the crumbs at the rich man's table. Instead, the dogs lick his sores. He is not welcome to sit and eat there. In Mark 7:25-28, a Gentile woman begs Jesus to drive a demon out of her daughter. When Jesus likens the woman to a dog, she tells him that even the dogs under the table eat the children's crumbs. He rewards her persistence and wisdom by healing her daughter. Alvin, my chipmunk, is persistent just like that woman who keeps after Jesus to heal her daughter. Alvin's reward is the food he gobbles up.

With new insight I re-evaluate my opinion of Alvin. The birds and chipmunk remind me that the next time an unwanted visitor comes to my bird feeder I shouldn't complain about it. Instead, I should be thankful for the food God provides for the small creatures and for me, in His Word.

Prayer: Dear God, thank you for your mercy to us as we are not unwanted guests at your table. You've included us through Jesus' death on the cross. All we need to do is seek you and accept your gift of salvation, just like Alvin accepts the food set out before him. Thank you for your gracious mercy. Amen.

Feeding and Praising Before the Storm

It's cold outside and snow is expected today. The birds seem to know it too. The black-capped chickadees, tufted titmice, and the white-breasted nuthatches vie for seeds at the bird feeder, seeking their fill before the storm. After them, the cardinals and then the woodpecker arrive.

It's a gray morning, without a glorious sunrise. Yet, as I sit and watch the birds and listen to the Psalms on my Bible app, I imagine the beginning of the song "When Morning Gilds the Sky."

Why would this old hymn come to mind on such a dreary day? I'm not sure. I look up facts about the song. It was written in German in the early 1800s and in 1854 translated by Edward Caswall into English.

I read the words to the song, "When morning gilds the sky, my heart awakening cries, may Jesus Christ be praised." This reminds me that the birds, in their own way praise God for their food, through their tweets, trills, and chirps. The song continues with the words "In all our work and prayer we ask his loving care: may Jesus Christ be praised." I realize I need to remember to ask God to direct my work and all I do.

Prayer: Dear God, just as the songwriter notes, I pray that this would be my own eternal song: "May Jesus Christ be praised." Thank you for listening, God. Amen.

Scattered Seeds on the Ground

Last night I saw the just-filled-to-the-top bird seed container was completely empty. This morning there are only piles of seeds scattered on the snowy ground. "That should be enough to get them through the day," I think as I sip my coffee and stare out at the scene.

Since our yard is enclosed with a nine-foot-high fence and there are no footprints around the feeder, I can only assume the birds in their frozen, frenzied flying and pecking for food at the bird feeder yesterday, have eaten and dropped seeds to the ground. It is very cold with windchills below zero degrees, so they are hungry.

This morning, I watch juncos, tufted titmice, black-capped chickadees, sparrows, cardinals, and a red-bellied woodpecker scrounge for food in the snow. The scattered seeds remind me of Bible verses God brings to my mind as I need them, scattering His hope and Word as morsels of encouragement and sustenance for my daily life. The only thing that is different from the birds' scenario of flitting to and fro, picking up seeds and sometimes fighting with other birds for them, is that I don't have to fight for His words of encouragement. In some countries people do. Where I live, all I need to do is open my Bible and read, letting God's Word refresh and strengthen my soul.

Isaiah 46:4 reminds me, "I am he who will sustain you." Isaiah 40:31 says, "But those who hope in the Lord will renew their strength. They will soar on wings like eagles, they will run and not grow weary, they will walk and not be faint." Likewise, Psalm 19:7 points out that "The Law of the Lord is perfect, refreshing the soul. The statutes of the Lord are trustworthy, making wise the simple."

Prayer: Dear God, help me to feed on your Word so that your law, your wisdom will flow through me like scattered seeds to feed my soul. Thank you. In Jesus' name I pray, Amen.

Carousel of Cares

The stage is set this late March morning. Alvin the chipmunk hunkers down within a flowerbed beneath the bird feeder, scratching for seeds. Black-capped chickadees, cardinals, and tufted titmice dart in and out at the other bird feeder, making it twirl first one way, then the other, reminding me of a carousel going round and round.

I'm gulping the last of my second cup of coffee before I dart off to the doctor. Do I have a cold, strep throat, or the flu? I don't know. I've had a low-grade fever all week and it's Friday so I need answers. I'm reminded of the Scripture in Matthew 7:7 that says, "Ask and it will be given to you, seek and you will find; knock and the door will be opened to you." I'm thankful there's a God who hears my cares and that I also was able to get a doctor's appointment. I'm going to hop on the carousel of wellness and get to my doctor, so I'll finish this later, just like the birds who dart in and out coming back for more food as they need it.

Prayer: Dear God, thank you that you care and thank you for my doctor's bronchitis diagnosis, and for the medication I need. Thank you for your provision of healing as I rest in you. In Jesus' name I pray, Amen.

Figure 2: Carousel of birds

Unadorned Like the Birds

I'm reading the Bible about King David's last days as king (1 Kings 9:1-31). It strikes me how mankind's habits and cultures shape the way we view and act around leaders. Richly dressed Bathsheba and plainly dressed Nathan the prophet bow down to the ground as they greet the king. This is high homage for a man who started out as a shepherd boy and became a warrior king.

As I sip my coffee, looking out at the birds at the feeder I am impressed with their simplicity. They wear the colors and feathers of their kind, unadorned with pomp or ceremonial clothes and customs.

Job 1:21 reminds me, "Naked I came from my mother's womb, and naked I will depart. The Lord gave and the Lord has taken away; may the name of the Lord be praised."

God knows who we are, our essence, as Psalm 139:13 says, "For you created my inmost being; you knit me together in my mother's womb." If God knows me, the real me, my thoughts, motivations, hopes and fears, and still loves me, why should I worry?

Prayer: Dear God, since my time on earth is spent developing into the person you would have me become, I pray that when I see you face to face, I am all you would have me be, shorn of the trappings of this world, fully centered on you. Thank you, Lord. Amen.

WAITING

Waiting Upon the Lord

I bring the bird feeder in almost every night because otherwise the deer eat all the seeds and have damaged it in the past. This morning, it is cold when I take the feeder outside. I shiver and rub my hands to warm them when I come back inside. Winter doesn't want to let go. I sit down to pray, eat my breakfast, and listen on my phone to my Bible app chapter for the day. I glance outside. No birds.

I finish eating, stack my dishes in the dishwasher, and get my second cup of coffee. No birds.

I sit down at the table and wait. Birds! Black-capped chickadees, house finches, and tufted titmice start flitting, hopping, and pecking for food. I ponder how often we wait... for God to hear us, to answer our prayers and to comfort us with His presence. Like my waiting for the birds to arrive, it takes time. When He, like the birds, appears, it is worth the wait.

Why should I wait upon the Lord? Scripture tells of many advantages and blessings that follow for those who wait upon the Lord.

1. He strengthens me:

   Psalm 27:14 says, "Wait for the Lord; be strong and take heart and wait for the Lord."

2. He renews and restores me:

   Isaiah 40:31 says: "But those who hope in the Lord will renew their strength. They will soar on wings like eagles; they will run and not grow weary; they will walk and not be faint."

3. He cleanses me of worry and anger:

Psalm 37:7-9 says: "Be still before the Lord and wait patiently for him; do not fret when people succeed in their ways, when they carry out their wicked schemes. Refrain from anger and turn from wrath; do not fret—it leads only to evil. For those who are evil will be destroyed, but those who hope in the Lord will inherit the land."

Psalm 37: 34 adds: "Hope in the Lord and keep his way. He will exalt you to inherit the land; when the wicked are destroyed, you will see it."

4. He listens and hears my cares:

Psalm 40:1, "I waited patiently for the Lord; he turned to me and heard my cry."

Knowing God hears me, listens, and helps me is important to remember. But how often do I wait upon the Lord? It makes me wonder. May I find joy in my waiting.

Prayer: God, help me to find time and the willingness to wait upon you so that I may hear you and renew my spirit to face the day and all that lies ahead, knowing you are in control. In Jesus' name I pray, Amen.

The Importance of Silence

It's a beautiful sunny morning. Blue skies beckon as I sit at my table waiting in silence for birds to come. I'm watchful and quiet, a lot like I should be as I wait upon the Lord. How often do I sit in silence? I drink my coffee and ponder. The world and its cares are knocking on the door of my mind, just like the beautiful day outside, but I wait in silence... and pray. "What would you have me do today, Father?"

The recent fighting in Ukraine comes to my mind. I recall the beginning of Psalm 46:10: "Be still and know that I am God." Is that all, God? What about the world? I sit, waiting. I feel Him saying, "I am with you in the turmoil, the raging tempest in the world. If I can count the hairs on your head, and know when even the littlest sparrow falls, I know what is happening to you and to all the others in the world. I am with you. I walk with you each and every day. So... be still and know that I am God."

The birds still haven't come to see if I've put out any food for them, but the sky is blue, and I know God is with me, and it is enough.

Prayer: Dear God, thank you that I can hear you in the silence. I pray those who struggle may feel your presence as you walk beside them this day, no matter where they are, no matter what they are doing. In Jesus' name I pray, Amen.

The Aha Moment

The past week or so I've been trying to identify the species of several birds at the feeder. I even post a picture on Facebook. Then I have an "aha" moment as I watch the antics of those below the bird feeder. The female cardinal keeps picking up a seed and feeding it to one of three hairless birds on the ground. Aha! The birds in question are baby cardinals newly out of their nest. Two of the three adapt quickly to getting their own food. The third one, however, shivers and the mother keeps feeding it. I have never seen a bird shiver before. It is fascinating yet worrisome. Is there something wrong with this particular bird? I watch the rest of the morning.

I also research to learn more about cardinals. I discover these three birds hatched about a month earlier and are now in the process of learning how to gather their own food.

But the shivering one worries me. It seems to need more help than the others. Will it grow stronger and be able to fend for itself this winter?

These birds remind me of people. We are all different. Some people learn faster and easier. Others need more support, just like the shivering baby cardinal.

Then I have another aha moment. Everyone needs help to grow as a Christian. I need help at times to understand God's word and grow in my faith. God is so patient, just like the mama cardinal is. His Word is constant and available for me to read and understand as I am ready to receive it.

Prayer: God, thank you for your patience, and for your Word that gives me food for my daily walk with you in the midst of my earthly travels. Abide with me and guide me through your Word and let your Holy Spirit encourage and reveal what you would have me understand as I grow in you. Amen.

You Finally Came to Eat

Whenever I bring in my bird feeder, I sprinkle the seeds that are left at the bottom of it in the grass for the mourning doves and other birds that like to eat from the ground. Then I can fill the feeder with fresh seeds. As I eat breakfast, I ask, "Where are the birds I usually see that come to eat from the ground? I set aside food especially for them."

I see the usual chipmunk gobbling up seeds from the grass as fast as he can. But that is all. Finally, toward the end of my meal I see one mourning dove swoop down and start to eat. I wonder why it didn't come earlier and eat more of the food set out especially for it.

Then it hits me. That's just like God and His Word. He has set aside Scripture for me to feast upon each morning, if only I stop and spend time with Him. As the mourning dove seeks seeds for sustenance, I am reminded in Matthew 5:6 that "Blessed are those who hunger and thirst for righteousness, for they shall be filled." The Hebrews are reminded in Jeremiah 3:15, "Then I will give you shepherds after my own heart, who will lead you with knowledge and understanding." The Scriptures feed me knowledge and the Holy Spirit gives me understanding. That is how I gain my heavenly food. Are you eating enough?

Prayer: Dear God, thank you that you provide for me and help me to feast on your Word. Like the birds of the air, you care for my physical and spiritual needs. May I be encouraged to set aside time to meet with you each morning and day as I grow in my faith and walk with you. In Jesus' name I pray, Amen.

Figure 3: Chipmunk visitor

What Happened at the Bird Feeder?

We have had some gray and windy days, but nothing prepares me for the sight awaiting me this morning. Once again, I forgot to bring in the bird feeder the night before. As I begin my breakfast, I see the feeder is missing four of the six perches at the openings. They lie scattered on the ground and the bird feeder is empty! One perch has been pecked off before, but not four of them. In addition, the bottom is tilting, as if it will fall off.

I look at the ground. Where are the piles of birdseed that would have poured out? Nothing.

Since we have a new, higher fence it isn't likely deer would have jumped over this nine-foot obstacle. The gates are secure as well. What has happened? I go outside to look. As I walk around the yard, I see patches of feathers lying in clumps in the grass. A small cluster of gray and white feathers banded together lie near the bird feeder, a few scattered feathers are farther along, then a large group of feathers are midway in the yard.

It must have happened suddenly during the night. The birds must have either fought something bigger than themselves or not known what was coming until it was too late.

The sudden disappearance and wreckage at the bird feeder makes me think of what Scriptures say about Christ's return. We will be caught unaware as well. Matthew 24:42-44 says, "Therefore keep watch, because you do not know on what day your Lord will come. But understand this: if the owner of the house had known at what time of night the thief was coming, he would have kept watch and would not have let his house be broken into. So you also must be ready, because the Son of Man will come at an hour when you do not expect him." Mark 13:32-33 says, "But about that day or hour no one knows, not even the angels in heaven, nor the Son, but only the Father. Be on guard! Be alert! You do not know when that time will come."

Prayer: Dear God, may my heart and mind rest in you, to grow in love and understanding of your Word so that I am ready when you come again. Amen.

Jumping Jacks

It's April and winter is slowly giving sway to spring. Flowers are budding and the birds are singing as they come to the feeders. All are in pairs, except for the lone chipmunk. Instead, it hops and jumps up and down from one flowerpot to another searching for seeds. A songbird sparrow is doing the same thing right now. These pots are right below one of the feeders and seeds fall into them. That's probably the reason the creatures are hopping in and out like jumping jacks between the pots.

Just as the chipmunk and the birds peck for seeds, I need to search for kernels of wisdom on how to live my life as well as how to prepare for eternity. As a snowbird, or junco, pecks below the bird feeder I think of how I need to dig for God's Word to guide me as I wait upon the Lord for an answer to a prayer I have about a novel I have sent to my agent.

During my devotion time I think about my writing, and I remember the battle belongs to the Lord. I look up that phrase in the Bible and find that there are numerous Scriptures (at least 100) where the Israelites and later Christians are reminded of this same thing. Whether it is a physical or mental battle, Scriptures in 1 Samuel 17:47, 2 Chronicles 20:15, Proverbs 21:31, Ephesians 6:12, 1 Corinthians 15:57, and Romans 8:37 tell me the victory lies with God. Exodus 14:14 tells me that the Lord will fight for me and I have only to be still. James 4:7 reminds me to submit myself to God, resist the devil and he will flee from me.

One of the most reassuring passages for me is Romans 8:31 which says, "What, then, shall we say in response to these things? If God is for us, who can be against us?" I read in Ephesians 6:10, "Finally be strong in the Lord and in his mighty power."

So when my thoughts do jumping jacks seeking peace, seeking answers, I know I need to dig into God's Word, and claim His strength and His might. Then when I pray and wait for Him to act, I'll know that in God's time, all will be done for His glory and in the best way possible for me as well.

Prayer: Dear God, thank you for listening. Thank you for your words of wisdom and unfailing love and faithfulness. I claim the victory for my prayers, and that you will fight the battle for me as I rest in you, and you will be victorious. In Jesus' name I pray, Amen.

Uncertainty

I see birds who come to the feeder continually glancing around with each peck for food. They act uncertain when they don't feel safe. In the past I've seen hawks swoop down to grab birds there. But not today. All is well.

Yet I know what it feels like to be uncertain. A red spot and lump on one of my breasts worries me. Two phone calls later, I have an appointment with my gynecologist. An exam and two medical scripts for diagnostic tests after that, I go home to wait. By the end of the week, I have the tests and the doctor tells me all looks fine. Nothing to worry about.

Aside from not sleeping well the night before the tests, I have peace. *God is with me, so I need not be afraid.* But I realize other women may not be as fortunate. I have three cousins who have fought Cancer and come through victorious, praise the Lord.

I have one more course of action to see to the end before I can put this episode behind me. However, the refrain of a song that was sung last Sunday in church keeps running through my mind, "You are not alone, God will go before you, you are not alone."

Just as the birds keep watch, I know it's important to do the same with my health. However, I know God holds me in the palm of His hand and walks with me in uncertain and unhappy times. I Peter 5:7 reminds me to cast all my cares and anxieties on Him, because He cares for me.

Prayer: Dear God, thank you for your love and care. Thank you, that you walk with me when I'm anxious or feeling uncertainty. I give my cares and concerns to you. In Jesus' name I pray, Amen.

PUTTING GOD FIRST

Clean-Up Day

It's raining outside. The warmer temperatures of the last few days have allowed the snow to melt, revealing a lot of seeds that have fallen from the bird feeder onto the ground. With the constant rain and mist rising from the colder ground, I decide to keep the bird feeder inside so that the birds can "clean up" the ground. Well, that and I don't want birdseed in the feeder to clump and stick inside.

Will any birds come to clean up? Will they even bother to show up in the steady downpour?

Ahh! I see a female cardinal, then a black-capped chickadee. Wait, there's a sparrow. A few minutes later, another black-capped chickadee swoops into view. They don't stay long, but they do eat what's down there. It may be slim pickings or the scarcity of a bountiful source of food in the woods that makes them resort to cleaning up the ground and gleaning the leftovers. Whatever the reason, there is just enough for them to live on.

It reminds me of the story of Ruth the Moabite daughter-in-law of Naomi, an Israelite widow. Ruth accompanies Naomi back to Israel. There, Naomi persuades Ruth to glean in a relative named Boaz's field. Gleaning grain to survive leads to a marriage proposal for Ruth. From scarcity to security.

How often do I find myself forced to glean to survive? Do I trust in God to see me through times when my bountiful supply is taken away?

Just as the birds focus on finding a source of food, I must focus on my source of hope and life. God reminds me in Matthew 6:26-27 to "Look at the birds of the air; they do not sow or reap or store away in barns, and yet your heavenly father feeds them. Are you not much more valuable than they? Can any one of you by worrying add a single hour to your life?"

Clean-up days in my life can also mean cleaning out closets, and rooms, getting rid of the detritus of life so that I have a clean place, uncluttered by items I don't need or use. My mind and spirit need clean-up days too. Then I can focus, like the birds do on their food, on my source of sustenance—God. Matthew 6:19-21 reminds me not to let my mind, or my heart be consumed by things of the world that can clutter my life. Instead, I need to keep my eyes on God, for where my treasure is, there my heart will be as well.

Prayer: Dear God, help me to not be anxious about my clean-up days, knowing you walk with me and provide for me just as you do the birds of the air. Help me to look around and see your provision and be thankful and at peace. In Jesus' name I pray, Amen.

Figure 4: Mourning dove clean-up

Flitter, Flutter Chickadee

This morning as I finish a cup of coffee and get ready for my day's activities, I notice a black-capped chickadee flitting and fluttering around the bird feeder. It is trying to figure out which opening to use to get the birdseed. This makes me wonder—how many times do I flit and flutter about choosing my activities during the day?

We all face times when we must make decisions, some not so important, others life changing. My decision to accept that Jesus died for my sins, made when I was about twelve years old, led me down a different path from many of my friends and family. I didn't realize it at the time, but since then, I know that God's protection surrounds me and He walks with me through every decision I make, no matter what I face.

Today, I try to remember, when I start to flit and flutter about decisions I must make, that God's got this. I just need to seek His help and guidance. Mathew 6:33 states, "But seek first His kingdom and His righteousness, and all these things will be given to you as well."

Prayer: Dear God, help me to always seek you first in all that I do. I praise you and thank you for your guidance. In Jesus' name, Amen.

Figure 5: Black-capped chickadee dance

The Case of the Missing Birdseed

The wind is blowing, and it's drizzling as I watch the black-capped chickadees and tufted titmice visit my bird feeder. Yesterday afternoon I filled the container to the very top. I forgot to bring it in at night, so this morning a third of the seed is missing. Gone. Did the birds eat it during the night or what?

I research and find there are two types of birds: Nocturnal (night feeding) ones, and Diurnal (morning and dusk feeding) ones. My birds are diurnal, although I see them at all hours of the day searching for food. Right now, it is almost 10:00 a.m. and the tufted titmice and black-capped chickadees are busy eating. Earlier, mourning doves grazed below the feeder.

But this doesn't answer my original question. Who or what ate the seeds during the night? Animals? The baffle, or cone around the shepherd's crook pole, should take care of little creatures. Deer? I haven't seen any traces of them for a while. Maybe I just missed the feeding frenzy earlier in the morning since I do not get up at dawn.

Watching the birds get their sustenance, I think of how each morning as I eat breakfast, I try to spend time feeding my spirit as I listen to God's Word. Unseen by the world, I find I need food for my day too.

I'm reminded of my favorite song, an African-American Spiritual titled "Give Me Jesus" which starts with the words: "In the morning when I rise... give me Jesus." So, like the birds I'll feed on Scriptures and meet Jesus in the morning and at night when I go to sleep.

Isaiah 26:3 says, "You will keep in perfect peace those whose minds are steadfast, because they trust in you." We are reminded that God, Himself, is steadfast in 2 Thessalonians 3:3. "But the Lord is faithful, and he will strengthen you and protect you from the evil one." Protection. That's the key. And that's one of the reasons birds eat when they do; they feel they are more protected at those times. We, like the birds, are mortal, so it is good to be reminded in Psalm 73:26, "My flesh and my heart may fail, but God is the strength of my heart and my portion forever." So, whenever we feel something is missing or lost, just like in the case of the missing birdseed, we can rest assured we live in God's protection and steadfast love.

Prayer: Dear God, thank you that you are my shield and sustenance. Thank you for your guidance as I feed on your words. Help me to know that I need not worry about things that disappear, but trust in you to provide for my needs. In Jesus' name I pray, Amen.

Figure 6: Downy woodpecker feeding

The Call of the Blue Jay

I hear the morning call of the blue jay as it swoops down to my bird feeder saying, "There's food for me, food I see." The blue jay's voice reminds me of myself. I'm a caller too.

In grade school, walkers were always dismissed a few minutes before the students who rode the bus home. We played a game, calling out when the bus was approaching us. I took pride in being the first to announce it. I had a loud voice so everyone could hear me when I called out, "B.U.S.—bus!"

It's laughable years later, but the uncanny resemblance to the blue jay worries me. Who wants to be a loudmouth? Not me. When I read up on blue jays, I learn they are intelligent, building strong familial ties with other blue jays. Hmm, not so bad. They live longer than other birds I see at my bird feeder, like the black-capped chickadees. I'll take the longer life span trait. I too try to foster strong ties within my family. So the comparison I find isn't all that bad.

Proverbs 18:21 says that death and life are held in the power of the tongue. Just like the blue jay calling out, "There's food," I need to call out that there is salvation in Jesus and that the Bible provides the food we need for our spirit to grow in our faith.

Prayer: Dear God, thank you for your gift of salvation through Jesus. Help me to call boldly like the blue jay that there's food for the Spirit found in God's word to those in need. In Jesus' name I pray, Amen.

Hungry Birds

The sun is shining, making it hard to believe the temperature is only in the 30s outside. Coming into my greatroom, I notice two tufted titmice in their usual spot, searching for food. Oops! No bird feeder. I still have to take it out this morning. I'm a little late as it's past 9:00 a.m.

I pick up the feeder. Hmm, only half-full and I just filled it the day before. I think my birds like to graze on food all day like my husband.

After setting it up, I retreat inside to continue my morning, and watch the birds. Sure enough, they come back. The tufted titmice think they own the place, the way they hover and swoop to eat.

As the morning continues, more birds come: a mourning dove, a red-bellied woodpecker, a downy woodpecker, a white-breasted nuthatch or two, the black-capped chickadees, and of course the female and male cardinals. Later, a sparrow joins the group, claiming and seeming to set up shop along the edge of one of my bird feeders, sampling the seeds.

The birds vie for their food, flitting and flying around the openings, sometimes taking turns nicely, other times knocking other birds off a perch. All in search of food.

Do we seek as earnestly for God's Word, our holy food? Our souls need it to grow in our faith. As I look around, I doubt it. I've had numerous conversations with people my age and younger who will admit they don't know much about the Scriptures. I was one of those people years ago. I'm so grateful I have time in retirement to spend each morning reading and listening to God's Word, my Holy food.

Prayer: Dear God, thank you for your Word, my daily bread for my soul. May I eagerly seek to be full of your wisdom, like the birds hungrily pecking and reaching for the seeds at the feeder. May I sup at your bird feeder, the Bible, and find sustenance for my soul. In Jesus' name I pray, Amen.

Figure 7: Hungry birds

Balmy Weather

I take the bird feeder out late in the morning and enjoy the balmy weather, wearing no coat, just a short-sleeved tee-shirt, jeans, and shoes. It almost smells like spring, but as the wind with its wintry bite reminds me, it's only late January. There's more winter weather ahead.

A few birds have come to the feeder, a big difference from two days earlier when they had a feeding frenzy. The good weather and smaller number of birds remind me of how I tend to be a fair-weather Christian, seeking the Lord when life's storms attack and going off on my own when all is well.

I need to be constant in my devotion to God, seeking His face and His Word. I Chronicles 16:11 says, "Look to the Lord and his strength; seek his face always." God promises in Proverbs 8:17 that those who seek Him will find Him. Matthew 7:7-8 tells me, "Ask and it will be given to you; seek and you will find; knock and the door will be opened to you. For everyone who asks receives, the one who seeks finds; and to the one who knocks, the door will be opened." And in Psalm 34:10 He says that those who seek the Lord lack no good thing.

Prayer: Dear God, help me to be constant in my devotion to you, seeking your face, your words and your will for my life during the storms and the balmy weather. In Jesus' name I pray, Amen.

Nocturnal Visitors

Out of curiosity this morning, I decide to check my phone to see what pictures my bird feeder camera may have taken overnight. I am shocked to see a furry body with long fingers or toes appear. Then, behind it, I see the image of a deer, its eyes reflecting the camera light in the darkness.

We have a nine-foot fence surrounding our backyard. I didn't think a deer could jump over it. But according to the picture it did. When I post the photograph on Facebook, I receive all sorts of guesses as to what the creature is. I lean toward it being a squirrel. Two days later another picture on the same camera shows the face of the creature reaching for seeds. It is a raccoon!

I'm reluctant to feed these nocturnal visitors so I'll have to make sure that any seeds I put in the blue bird feeder are eaten during the day with none left over at night. I already take the other bird feeder inside when it gets dark, but the one the animals are visiting is attached to my deck railing. Maybe filling that feeder half full early in the morning will ensure that it's empty come nighttime. I'll have to see.

There's another thing I need to make sure of—I need to find time to be with God and read His Word. It's been a crazy week, so I haven't been as diligent as I'd like in my devotions. Proverbs 4:23 reminds me to guard my heart, for everything I do flows from it. So, when I get off track, or get disturbed by strange, nocturnal visitors at my bird feeder, I can rest, believing and knowing that God's got this, He's in control. As Hebrews 11:6 says, "And without faith it is impossible to please God, because anyone who comes to Him must believe that He exists and that He rewards those who earnestly seek Him." My reward for believing in God and seeking Him, is peace. His peace.

Prayer: Dear God, forgive me when I let things of the world scare or upset me. Help me to be diligent and seek you and your peace, putting you first. Thank you that I can come to you with my care. In Jesus' name I pray, Amen.

The Pitter Patter of Perseverance

Pitter patter, what's that I see? A tiny bird, the chickadee. The sight of the cheerful bird brings this rhyme to my mind and makes me smile at what I find. Next comes a pair of blue jays, then a wren and chipmunk all happily munching on seeds. Later a sparrow and a rose-breasted grosbeak peck for food around the bird feeder. And still, the rain comes sprinkling down, so lightly it is hard to see except for the effect it has on the puddles on my deck.

The hardiness and perseverance of the birds as they obtain food despite the weather or other circumstances reminds me that I, like the birds, need to persevere in growing my faith and knowledge of the Lord. King Solomon writes much about seeking wisdom in Proverbs. For instance, Proverbs 9:10 says, "The fear of the Lord is the beginning of wisdom, and knowledge of the Holy One is understanding." Solomon continues to remind me in Proverbs 3:5-6, "Trust in the Lord with all your heart and lean not on your own understanding; in all your ways submit to him, and he will make your paths straight."

In my daily devotions I try to do as Solomon wrote in Proverbs 23:12, "Apply your heart to instruction and your ears to words of knowledge."

Prayer: Dear God, thank you for your Word, your Holy Spirit and guidance I find as I read the Bible. Thank you for helping me persevere in hard times, trusting you to lead me where I ought to go. In Jesus' name I pray, Amen.

GOD'S LOVE

The Pecking Order

As I watch the various birds flit to our feeder, I'm struck by how differently they act. Today, the house finches and sparrows scavenge for seed in the snow below the feeder, only rarely popping up to it for food. The titmice, chickadees, and white-breasted nuthatches wait, perching on other places until it's their turn. Occasionally they flutter wings at each other if one bird encroaches on another's opportunity to feed. But they all give way to the larger birds like the cardinals and blue jays. The mourning doves search the ground, seeking seeds and insects alike.

The pecking order at the bird feeder is a symphony of size, speed, and time accompanied by the chirps, cheeps, tweets, and trills of their calls. It's a microcosm of how humans live their lives. Some people are at the top of the pecking order because of wealth, position, or power while others range lower in the order. But all of us, just like those birds at the feeder, have our place of equal value to God who loves and provides for us all.

Taking the advice found in Matthew 6:26 and 31-34, I learn I should not worry about the world's pecking order. When I feel anxious, angry, or bitter about my life, I must remember God cares for me.

Matthew 6:26 says, "Look at the birds of the air; for they do not sow or reap or store away in barns, and yet your heavenly Father feeds them. Are you not much more valuable than they?" While this Scripture should not make me complacent, it should empower me to be the best I can be in an unfair world running contrary to God's Word. For He is with me. Matthew 6:31-34 reminds me: "So do not worry, stating, 'What shall we eat?' or 'What shall we drink?' or 'What shall we wear?' For the pagans run after all these things, and your heavenly Father knows that you need them. But seek first his kingdom and his righteousness, and all these things will be given to you as well. Therefore, do not worry about tomorrow, for tomorrow will worry about itself. Each day has enough trouble of its own."

Prayer: God, walk with me and bear my burdens each day. I trust in your care and love, knowing you will meet my needs. When I start to doubt or look around me at what is happening in the world or in my own life, help me to trust you are with me and will lift my cares from my shoulders and guide me. In Jesus' name I pray, Amen.

A Stranger Appears

It is a busy day outside my window, but that doesn't stop a strange large bird from swooping in and angling its body so it can reach into the feeder. While it is there, the song sparrow pecks in the snow, and the tufted titmice and black-capped chickadees flit and loop around, waiting for their chance. Later, the downy woodpecker takes a turn, while the cardinal stands its ground below. The stranger, in this case a wren, doesn't stay long. But this occurrence does make me wonder—if birds welcome strangers, sharing their food, why don't humans? Why don't we welcome the alien among us?

While a stranger is someone we don't know, the term *alien* seems to distance us even further from that individual. In biblical terms, it shouldn't. Throughout the Old and New Testaments, it tells us to be helpful to strangers for many reasons.

1. God reminds Abraham and the Israelites that they were strangers in a foreign land. In Genesis 23:4 Abraham acknowledges, "I am a foreigner and a stranger among you. Sell me some property for a burial site here so I can bury my dead." Deuteronomy 10:19 says, "And you are to love those who are foreigners, for you yourselves were foreigners in Egypt." Leviticus 19:34 admonishes us about how we should act. "The foreigner residing among you must be treated as your native-born. Love them as yourself, for you were foreigners in Egypt. I am the Lord your God."

2. When we help the least among us, we are helping God. Matthew 25:35 explains: "For I was hungry and you gave me something to eat, I was thirsty and you gave me something to drink, I was a stranger and you invited me in."

3. We should help other believers. Matthew 25:40 continues addressing how we should help and why. "Truly I tell you, whatever you did for one of the least of these brothers and sisters of mine, you did for me." Romans 12:13 tells us: "Share with the Lord's people who are in need. Practice hospitality."

4. We may be entertaining angels when we help a stranger. Hebrews 13:1-2 says, "Keep on loving one another as brothers and sisters. Do not forget to show hospitality to strangers, for by so doing some people have shown hospitality to angels without knowing it."

Just like the birds in my yard we show love by being helpful to the strangers among us.

Prayer: Dear God, help me to be open to help and guide the strangers I encounter during my day. Help me to show your love and acceptance as I meet others daily. In Jesus' name I pray, Amen.

Diversity

Black-capped chickadees, red-headed finches, songbird finches, sparrows, juncos, red-bellied woodpeckers, two male and two female cardinals, a downy woodpecker, and a blue jay all arrive today. There is such diversity at the bird feeder! They wait turns, occupying different places, all vying for seeds. Oops, a mourning dove just dropped in. And here comes the white-breasted nuthatch.

Seeing such a variety of birds makes me think of how God delights in all his creatures. With multitudes of different birds, insects, animals and plants and fish in our world, how can He not delight in diversity, in differences?

Mankind, however, does not. We separate and segregate people. I can't help wondering what we miss when we don't celebrate and rejoice in our differences. If the creator of everything celebrates and takes delight in differences, we should too. Little children delight in differences. We should be more like them. In Matthew 19:14 Jesus says, "Let the little children come to me and do not hinder them, for the kingdom of heaven belongs to such as these."

Prayer: Dear God, help me to delight in your diversity in this world, in all you've created. Help me to be kind to others who are different. Help me to enjoy the small things in life, resting in the knowledge that you care for each one of us, no matter how different we are. In Jesus' name I pray, Amen.

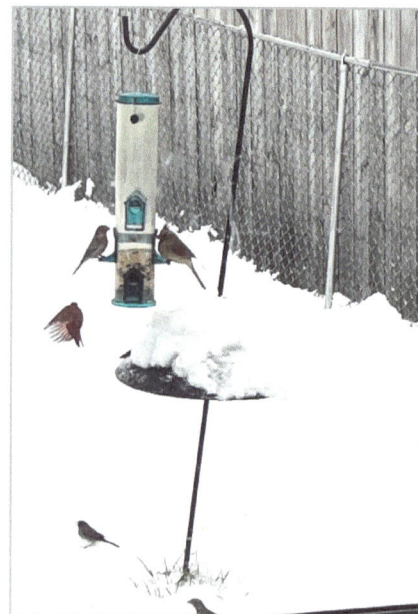

Figure 8: Winter wonderland variety

Rainy Days

Even on gray and rainy days, I can find joy if I remember the depths of God's love. John 3:16 tells me, "For God so loved the world that he gave his one and only Son, that whoever believes in him shall not perish but have eternal life."

In addition to His love, we have His peace. Isaiah 26:3 says, "You will keep in perfect peace those whose minds are steadfast, because they trust in you." John 14:27 adds, "Peace I leave with you; my peace I give you. I do not give to you as the world gives. Do not let your hearts be troubled and do not be afraid." As I think of these Scriptures, a poem comes to mind, and it is written below.

What's that bright red spot I see?

Heavenly messengers surrounding me.

Cardinal bright in rain sodden grass,

God's beacon of light as he does pass.

Drops spatter down and all around,

Birds forage for food where it can be found.

Gray skies encompass budding branches above,

Joy floods my soul with God's Holy Love.

Prayer: Dear God, help me to know you are with me even on gray, cold, dreary days. Help me to remember your love and to trust you and walk with you in all my ways. Amen.

Stare-Down

As I drink the last of my coffee, I watch two birds at the feeder. My eyes widen and I take a closer look. A female cardinal sits on one of the perches, wings puffed up to make her twice as big as she stares down another bird on the other side of the feeder. This incident lasts for thirty seconds, then apparently satisfied that boundaries have been set, the two eat in peace opposite each other.

How often do I puff myself up to appear more important to others? I notice red-winged black birds doing the same thing. Maybe birds aren't that different from me when I want to protect myself, so I seem important or to attract attention. The peacock male flaunts his finery when he spreads his colorful wings to attract the female. Turkeys puff themselves up and strut around, wings spread wide when they are courting females. I laugh at the comparisons.

May I always remember that even if people don't notice me, God does, and He cares for me. He also delights in me. Jeremiah 9:23-24 says, " 'Let not the wise boast of their wisdom or the strong boast of their strength or the rich boast of their riches, but let the one who boasts boast about this: that they have the understanding to know me, that I am the Lord who exercises kindness, justice and righteousness on earth, for in these I delight,' declares the Lord."

Prayer: God, just as you say in Isaiah 49:16, you have engraved my name on your hands, I pray your love and protection will help me realize I can go to you when I am troubled or threatened. May I know that you love me and hold me in the palm of your hand. Amen.

Figure 9: Stare-down at the bird feeder

He Knows My Name

I listen to Scriptures on my Bible app as I eat breakfast and stare out the window. A cardinal darts to the bird feeder, then a red-winged black bird. Last, but not least, a red-headed finch comes. Their personalities are so different, matching their appearance. I chuckle at how the finch manages to keep out of the larger bird's sight. Under the radar, again. The finches know how to hide and get what they want.

Then the Scriptures catch my attention. In Numbers, chapters 1 through 11, God tells Moses which men are to lead the Israelites as they go forth across the desert. He names specific men from each tribe. I am awestruck by the honor God gives the men. He knows each man's name and is specific as to what they are to do, both in numbering the people and in leading each group forth. Even though they are not necessarily famous to their peers, they are well-known to God.

We are told in Luke 12:6-7 that even though five sparrows may be sold for two pennies, God has not forgotten them. In addition, God has counted the very hairs on my head, and I am worth more than many sparrows. What an honor, that God loves me so much and knows me so well, that despite my flaws and weaknesses He is there walking with me. He knows my name.

Prayer: Dear God, thank you for guiding me and walking beside me. Help me to give praise to you. You are holy, you are loving. I thank you, that despite my weakness and sins, you care, that you are with me at all times. In Jesus' name, I praise you and thank you that you know my name. Amen.

Cowbirds Return

The cowbirds are back. They are not pretty birds, with their glossy black bodies and brown heads. They are similar in size to cardinals, but there the similarity ends. Cowbirds are considered brood parasites, using nests of other birds and laying their eggs so those birds will take care of the babies when they hatch. Their clucking sounds and short tweets or whistles may attract other cowbirds, even though their calls are not very loud. Three of them cluster at the different openings of one feeder and another perches on my camera feeder, shooing away other birds for a while. I try to scare them away so the chickadees and tufted titmice can eat. They fly away and then a few minutes later they return. Like the black-capped chickadees, the cowbirds are pesky, and persistent.

As I write this, I think of how I attribute the word 'pesky' to these birds, but not to the black-capped chickadees and tufted titmice who are also persistent. The reason? I don't find the cowbirds cute like the other ones.

How often do I use negative words to describe a person or object I may not like? It makes me pause and think. All living things are God's and have their own purpose. Who am I to judge and consider their worth less than another? If the creator shows no partiality (see Romans 2:11), why should I? James 2:8-9 goes further when talking about our relationships to each other: "If you really keep the royal law found in Scripture, 'Love your neighbor as yourself', you are doing right. But if you show favoritism, you sin and are convicted by the law as lawbreakers."

Prayer: Dear God, help me to be kind in my words and thoughts to others who are different from me. Help me to show your love and kindness to all creatures, great and small. In Jesus' name I pray, Amen.

Playing Leap-frog

Young children play leap-frog, one person crouching down while another jumps over him or her and so forth. I never expected to see a chipmunk leap over a cardinal and for that startled male to then leap over the female cardinal.

Crouching and leaping. Back and forth. I can't picture myself, at seventy, doing that. At least not physically. That makes me think. Do I play leap-frog with my life or my faith? Do I crouch down to make myself small or invisible or leap over a problem to escape dealing with it?

The Bible tells me that God is with me. He sees and cares for me, I need not fear the terror of the night, nor the arrow that flies by day (Psalm 91:5). In addition, God knows the plans He has for me, plans to prosper me and not to harm me, plans to give me hope and a future (Jeremiah 29:11). So, I don't need to play leap-frog to get away or to hide from trouble.

Instead, I can leap ahead joyfully in faith, knowing God is in control and will guide me in all my ways.

Prayer: Dear God, thank you for your love, for your Holy Spirit to guide me and most of all, thank you for the gift of salvation through Jesus Christ, your Son. Thank you for walking with me as I go about my day, whether I leap like the chipmunk and birds or walk, praising you. In Jesus' name I pray, Amen.

SEEKING GOD'S WILL

Look Up

There's a lot of snow around today, but the full bird feeders are clear of it. A few juncos peck at fallen seeds lying lightly on mounds of snow. The tufted titmice and blue jay eat the seeds on the platform of one of the feeders. A red cardinal eats up there too, taking turns. But the female cardinal and the juncos haven't—content, I assume, to forage for the scraps below.

The scene makes me think of myself and of others who sometimes are content with scraps of information, of Scriptures and fellowship with other believers. We don't look up to the source of it all—God.

I wrote a song once where the refrain was, "Look up, look up, look up. But God, which way is up?" 1 Chronicles 16:11 says, "Look to the Lord and his strength; seek his face always." Psalm 105:4 tells me to always seek His face and His strength. Jeremiah 29:13 and Deuteronomy 4:29 both assure me if I seek the Lord with my whole heart and soul, I will find Him. I need to remember and claim these promises. There are many more Scriptures that remind us to seek God, but Psalm 121: 1-8, a song of ascents, sums it up well. "I lift up my eyes to the mountains— where does my help come from? My help comes from the Lord, the Maker of heaven and earth. He will not let your foot slip—he who watches over you will not slumber; indeed, he who watches over Israel will neither slumber nor sleep. The Lord watches over you—the Lord is your shade at your right hand; the sun will not harm you by day, nor the moon by night. The Lord will keep you from all harm—he will watch over your life; The Lord will watch over your coming and going both now and forevermore."

Prayer: Dear God, please walk with me and guide me in the path I should follow, to know when and where to look up to you for your loving guidance. Help me to go to your Holy Scriptures to gain understanding of how, where, and when to look up to you, the source of everything. Amen.

Early Birds

I am up early today. Much earlier than usual, to help a friend. So, I put the bird feeder out earlier too.

As I eat after my morning prayer, I see several birds. Of course, the persistent black-capped chickadee pops in first, then a tufted titmouse. Most surprising of all though is my first sighting this winter of a red-bellied woodpecker! A few minutes later a cardinal appears ready to spar with a house finch over fallen seeds. Then, a white-breasted nuthatch loops into view. As I finish my bible study a junco arrives. Not a bad early morning view of birds such as the red-bellied woodpecker and the junco that I haven't seen since last winter.

In some ways, I liked to be early, or rather on time. As a student, whenever I had projects, I preferred being an early bird, getting things done way before the deadline so that if I had a problem or needed more time, I had peace of mind. That's what being an early bird gave me then and gives me now.

An early riser, however, I'm not. My body just doesn't like it. Today, I'm glad I did. In Psalm 119:147, King David alludes to his time full of strife and the importance of his early morning prayer to cry to God for help. He says, "I rise before dawn and cry for help; I have put my hope in your word."

Are you an early bird? What do you see when you're an early bird?

No matter what time of day you greet the Lord, whether as an early bird or later, it is good to meet Him and to watch, listen, and pray, to let God guide you in all His ways.

Prayer: God, thank you that you are here for me. Help me to seek you, to listen and to give you my cares for the day so that you may guide me in all my ways. Amen.

Good Morning, Chickadees

I put out the bird feeder and am getting ready to eat my breakfast when I see the bird—a black-capped chickadee. As soon as the words, "Good morning, chickadee," fly out of my mouth I think—that's how God would like me to greet Him and He would greet me!

What's a greeting? After all, I do it every day to my husband, or in this case to the birds. When I look it up, I read that it's an acknowledgment that another person is in your presence or it's a way of showing recognition or welcome. It's also a way to make the acquaintance of someone, or an expression of goodwill.

I use it verbally and in written forms. Verbally it's in my speech, whether it's my conversation or in my song.

When I sing praises to God and when I pray, I am greeting God. So, what is my manner of greeting someone? Is it friendly or harping or demanding, or complaining?

My mother used to say ASATAW, meaning a soft answer turns away wrath. It was her way of quoting from Proverbs 15:1 to me and my sisters when we were yelling or fighting with each other. That makes me think. How much better is a soft, gentle, or joyous greeting than a demanding one? In Psalms, David greets God with praises. Psalm 100:1-2 starts out, "Shout for joy to the Lord, all the earth. Worship the Lord with gladness; come before him with joyful songs." It continues to state how I should enter into God's presence in verse 4. "Enter his gates with thanksgiving and his courts with praise; give thanks to him and praise his name." I notice that it doesn't necessarily say I am praising Him for my situation, I am praising God for who He is. Psalm 95:1-2 says, "Come let us sing for joy to the Lord; let us shout aloud to the Rock of our salvation. Let us come before him with thanksgiving and extol him with music and song." Then Psalm 95:3-7 gives me reasons why I should praise Him, extol his greatness and His mighty works, and acknowledge Him as my creator.

When I greet God with praise, I open myself to His blessing. Even in distress, I should remember to praise God for who He is. The act of greeting with praise lets the Holy Spirit refresh and guide me in the day ahead.

When King Hezekiah is threatened by Sennacherib, King of Assyria, he prays to God. Is his greeting demanding, proclaiming fear and woe? No. He greets God with praise, lauding God as the living God of Israel. After he finishes praising God, he lays out the threat, then closes with a reminder of God's power, protection, and grace. (See Kings 19:14-19 and II Chronicles 32:20-22.)

In Psalms, we see that many times David praises God first before making requests for deliverance from evil. In Psalm 30, David extols God's greatness and how He delivered David from his enemies. But praise came before requests. No matter what your day may bring or what difficulties you may face, greet God and let Him, through His Holy Spirit, dwell in you and walk with you; learn to greet God with praise.

Prayer: God, thank you for being the Great I Am. For creating me, for creating the birds of the air, the creatures on land and sea. Thank you for being in control of my life, even when I don't see it. God, help me to greet you with praise. Teach me to worship you for who you are, first, so that my eyes may see, and my spirit know, what to seek in your will through whatever I face in the days ahead. In Jesus' name I pray, Amen.

Lord of the Seeds

This morning, I watch a very fat sparrow claim its territory among the birdseed, chasing after other birds who want to feast on the fallen kernels. Its belligerent attitude and unwillingness to share surprise me. I don't know if the 1-degree temperature and frozen snow have anything to do with this aggression.

Then I realize I am like the sparrow. I claim my rights, property, objects, and people as my own, with arrogant, aggressive behavior too. Black Friday comes to mind with angry shoppers and frustrated drivers honking their horns.

At times like these I should remember God will provide the things and people I need when I need them. I don't have to be like this sparrow, the lord of the seeds. God will take care of me. Philippians 4:19 says, "And my God will supply every need according to his riches in glory in Christ Jesus."

I don't have to hoard or worry about tomorrow. Jeremiah 29:11 says, "For I know the plans I have for you, declares the Lord, plans to prosper you and not to harm you, plans to give you hope and a future."

Matthew 6:25-34 reminds me to give my cares to God. "Therefore, I tell you, do not worry about your life, what you will eat or drink; or about your body, what you will wear. Is not life more than food, and the body more than clothes? Look at the birds of the air; they do not sow or reap or store away in barns, and yet your heavenly Father feeds them. Are you not much more valuable than they are? Can anyone of you by worrying add a single hour to your life? And why do you worry about clothes? See how the flowers of the field grow. They do not labor or spin, yet I tell you that not even Solomon in all his splendor was dressed like one of these."

The key to not feeling like the lord of the seeds is to do as John 15:7 says. "If you remain in me (Jesus) and my words (Scripture) remain in you, ask whatever you wish, and it will be done for you." Abiding in the Word helps me see as God sees so that what I ask for aligns with His will. Psalm 37:1-5 offers comfort and advice, so I am not like the sparrow, being lord of the seeds. "Do not fret because of those who are evil or be envious of those who do wrong; for like the grass they will soon wither, like green plants they will soon die away. Trust in the Lord and do good: dwell in the land and enjoy safe pasture. Take delight in the Lord, and he will give you the desires of your heart. Commit your way to the Lord; trust in him and he will do this."

Prayer: Dear God, thank you for your Word which comforts and guides me. Help me to not be lord of the seeds in my life but to trust you in and for all things. In Jesus' name I pray, Amen.

Ground Feeders

This morning, I once again sit and watch the birds at the feeder. Well, not actually at it, rather, below it. They are busily hunting and pecking the newly sprouting grassy ground in search of seeds and nuts, oblivious to the waiting feast above their heads (and not out of their reach) in the bird feeder.

It strikes me how often I search and hunt for my own food—my daily sustenance—never looking up to God for His bounty, waiting and ready for me through prayer and His Word. I Kings 17 tells how Elijah the Tishbite from Gilead has to rely on God's provision to survive. God sends Elijah into hiding from King Ahab using ravens to bring bread and meat to him each morning and night until the brook dries up. After that God tells him to seek a widow in Sidon who will supply him with food. In all this, Elijah has to trust in the Lord to provide. Philippians 4:19 comforts me with these words: "And my God will meet all your needs according to the riches of his glory in Christ Jesus."

Prayer: Dear God, help me to look to you, the source of all I need to nourish my soul. Help me to seek you in prayer and in your Word. In Jesus' name I pray, Amen.

Seeing Old Friends

I love sitting at my table watching my feathered friends come to the bird feeder right outside my window. Today as I watch a white-breasted nuthatch feed, contentment and happiness well up inside me. Viewing the birds come is like seeing and greeting old companions. I know I occasionally point out newcomers to the feeder, but seeing the regular visitors is like meeting up with old friends. Peace, joy, and contentment flood my soul. It reminds me, later today I will see my other old friends when we meet for lunch. After years of just writing notes on Christmas cards, we have re-connected in person. We will meet for lunch and catch up on all our activities since the last time we were together.

In the same way, I think I've gotten and am still getting to know God and His Son, Jesus, through reading the Bible. Each day I am deepening my relationship with Him. If I feel peace, joy, and contentment when I see my earth-bound friends, I can only imagine how wonderful it will be when I see God and His Son Jesus, face-to-face. What awesomeness awaits!

Hebrews 9:28 says, "so Christ was sacrificed once to take away the sins of many; and he will appear a second time, not to bear sin, but to bring salvation to those who are waiting for him." Isaiah 35:10 describes the joy we will have when Jesus returns for us. "And those the Lord has rescued will return. They will enter Zion with singing; everlasting joy will crown their heads. Gladness and joy will overtake them, and sorrow and sighing will flee away." As I write these words, I can hear a song I used to sing years ago that is based on this Scripture. I loved the song ("Therefore the Redeemed of the Lord Shall Return" by Ruth Lake, 1972) fifty years ago and it still resonates in my heart today.

Like a final homecoming, I read Romans 14:17. "For the kingdom of God is not a matter of eating and drinking, but of righteousness, peace and joy in the Holy Spirit." I love how God reminds me of what is to come with the sights I see at the bird feeder.

Prayer: Dear God, help me to carry the contentment I feel seeing old avian and human friends just as I have the sure knowledge and thankfulness that I will someday see you and your Son Jesus. I pray others may know and accept your saving grace so that they, like me, will be able to greet you as a dear friend in heaven. Amen.

Picky Eater

A white-breasted nuthatch picks and chooses the seeds it wants this morning. It reminds me of my oldest son and my grandsons. Such picky eaters! Every family has them. My mother was one too.

Why are we picky eaters? Is it the taste? Texture, appearance of the food or what? I'm not sure what the white-breasted nuthatch wants, but it comes back repeatedly for food, so I guess it finds what it desires or needs.

As a Christian I know I should feed on the Word of God. Not literally, but figuratively, so that Scripture is in my heart and in my mind. I've mentioned the African Spiritual "Give Me Jesus" before. The lyrics talk about various times of day when the singer seeks Jesus. The words make me think of the times of the day when I look for Jesus. The melody flows through my mind as I gaze out at the bird feeder and think of that white-breasted nuthatch. "In the morning when I rise, in the morning when I rise, in the morning when I rise, give me Jesus." The tune continues, so appropriate for my own thoughts—"and when I am alone, oh, and when I am alone, oh when I am alone, give me Jesus." The song crescendos with "And when I come to die, oh, and when I come to die. Oh, and when I come to die, give me Jesus." To me, this song sums up what I need to pick and choose the most, to seek for and to ask for, more of Jesus.

So, like the picky eater at the bird feeder, I'll just feed on God's word, in the morning, when I'm alone, and in the evening, to learn more of and to seek more of Jesus.

Prayer: Dear God, thank you for giving me your son Jesus. Thank you for meeting me when and where I am, to love me and guide me. In Jesus' name I pray, Amen.

It's All in the Perspective

It's a sunny summer morning and the chipmunk is at it again: eating the seeds I had scattered on the ground for the mourning doves. The next thing I know it jumps up onto the large flowerpot near the bird feeder. "It's going to dig at the roots of the flowers," I think. But no, it turns and perches on the edge of the flowerpot, gazing down at the bricks below. I look closer. A moment later it jumps down and scoops up a seed. A higher perch gives the chipmunk perspective to see what is hidden from other viewers like me.

I often need to perch high or step back to get a different view of my problems. No matter how I do it, God steps with me and helps me. 1 Corinthians 13:12 describes how that works: "For now we see only a reflection as in a mirror; then we shall see face to face. Now I know in part; then I shall know fully, even as I am fully known."

Since I know God walks with me and guides me, I need to ask for His perspective to see and meet the obstacles I face, just like the tufted titmouse and other birds that perch high above the bird feeder, and the chipmunk looking down from the flowerpot to the ground. I must perch high in God's Word and let the Holy Spirit guide me.

Prayer: Thank you, God, that you give me perspective and guidance to face my daily problems. Thank you, that I can surrender my cares to you and walk by faith, knowing you are in control. In Jesus' name I pray, Amen.

Figure 10: Chipmunk's perspective

Watery View

Today I am disappointed to see the night's dew misting my window view of the action of birds at my feeder. How can I tell which bird is which through the window? Then I think of the Bible verse in 1 Corinthians 13:12 which states, "For now we see only a reflection as in a mirror, then we shall see face to face. Now I know in part; then I shall know fully, even as I am fully known."

As the sun shines, my window view will clear, and I'll be able to see the birds more distinctly. But my view of God and His will, I only see in part, and that dimly. In order to know God more fully, I must go to my "bird feeder"—the Bible—to learn of Him.

In all my observations at the bird feeder I ask questions and find answers in the Bible. It amazes me that all nature sings, and His glory points us back to Him and His Word. All I need to do is look.

Prayer: Dear God, help me to seek you first and lean not on my own understanding, but to acknowledge you in all my ways. For you see clearly and know my going out and coming in. Thank you. In Jesus' name, Amen.

The Lamppost

The lamppost in the Narnia Chronicles by C. S. Lewis shows travelers the way to and from Narnia. On dark and snowy nights, the children who have gone to Narnia need a light to show them where to go. My bird feeder isn't a light, but it beckons birds to come and eat. When I fill the tube where they get their seeds, all sorts of birds flit around the feeder, vying for their portion on this bright summer day.

The Bible is like the bird feeder and the lamppost. When I read, I acquire food for the soul, God's wisdom, and sustenance for me, and light for my life. But do I avail myself of this food?

I watch my avian visitors continue to come even when the seed level gets low. The black-capped chickadee is one of the smallest of the visitors. When the seed becomes a little mound in the middle of the bottom of the feeder the bird still tries to get the food, perching half in and half out of the lowest opening. In fact, one time I had to open the tube to allow a trapped black-capped chickadee to escape.

I wonder, do I immerse myself in the Word of God, in my faith—sacrificing possible freedom for the opportunity to feed upon God's Word? Some people do, especially in countries that have no freedom of religion, where they risk being persecuted for their faith.

I should be more like the black-capped chickadee, fueling myself with God's Word so that I may be a beacon of hope in a dark and hungry world.

Prayer: Dear God, thank you for your Word, a lamp to light my way and provide food for my soul. I pray for those who suffer persecution when others try to squash and eliminate their light and spirits. May I be a lamp lit for your glory, to show others your way. Thank you for feeding me at your lamppost, the Bible. Just as you care for the birds, you care for me. I pray in Jesus' name, Amen.

Figure 11: Bird feeder as a lamppost

Almost Empty Bird Feeder and Me

The almost empty bird feeder right outside my greatroom window reminds me of myself. Like it, I'm in need of filling too, with daily sustenance, physically and spiritually. When I read Scriptures or do a Bible study as I am right now, using *The Discipline of Grace* by Jerry Bridges (1994), I'm reminded of one truth, or should I say, one fear I have. What I read needs to be remembered and acted upon, yet I'm afraid. Afraid I will take it in, then as the days and weeks go by, I'll forget the lessons or let my life resume its usual path.

And why is that bad, you ask?

Well, it means I've forgotten what I've learned, what in essence, has humbled me. Jesus warns His disciples in Matthew 13:18-22 of unfruitful seeds. He says, "Listen then to what the parable of the Sower means: When anyone hears the message about the kingdom and does not understand it, the evil one comes and snatches away what was sown in their heart. This is the seed sown along the path. The seed falling on rocky ground refers to someone who hears the word and at once receives it with joy. But since they have no root, they last only a short time. When trouble or persecution comes because of the word, they fall away. The seed falling among the thorns refers to someone who hears the word but the worries of this life and deceitfulness of wealth choke the word making it unfruitful."

I savor my last gulp of coffee and grip my hands, as I remind myself of my past experiences, then close my eyes in prayer.

Prayer: Dear God, please don't let your words, your wisdom, your teachings fall by the wayside like in the parable of the Sower. May your wisdom NOT be choked out or crowded out by the thorns of everyday concerns or get trampled on the stoney path of reality. Create a new and clean spirit within me, O Lord, and renew a right spirit within me. Amen.

Reaching Up

It's a gray spring morning as I look out at the bird feeder. A red-winged blackbird pecks at some seeds as a male cardinal scrounges below; its vivid red feathers against the green grass and plants remind me of Christmas.

One particular bit of grass catches my eye. I can't tell if it's a weed or a flower stem reaching up to the baffle on the tall metal hook that the feeder hangs upon. It reminds me of some plants I put under another bird feeder I have. I thought I'd transplanted hosta but their long leafy stems do not resemble hosta at all. Both plants are growing tall, reaching up, seeking sunlight. The plants remind me of little children in God's Garden reaching out for love and life. Both plants and children will be buffeted by the winds of strife and tears like raindrops falling on the ground.

People train plants as they grow, with their placement and strings or ties to hold them up. Proverbs 22:6 says, "Start children off in the way they should go, and even when they are old they will not turn from it."

Plants and children need loving care, just as the birds at the feeder do. Right now, a female cardinal is breakfasting. The sun is trying to burn away the cloud cover and the plants are growing. Psalm 127:3 reminds me that children are a heritage from the Lord, a reward from him. Just as I tend the birds at the feeder and watch the plants grow around it, I need to tend my garden of family, providing what they need, when they need it. At other times I must remember to sit back like I do at my table by the window, to enjoy the view before me. Most importantly, no matter how many family cares I have, I need to pray that God waters me, and helps me tend my own soul's garden so I grow in Him.

Prayer: Dear God, help me to tend my gardens, at the bird feeder, with my family and within myself with the light and love you have so freely given me in Christ Jesus, your son. Amen.

Faithful Black-capped Chickadees

It's a nice day, although gray clouds are gathering, blotting out the bright sunshine from earlier in the morning. As I look out the window, I see two black-capped chickadees pecking for seeds. They are one of the first birds I see when I first set out a bird feeder. Faithful, persistent, and plucky is how I would describe them. They'll hover near my bird feeders, then dart in to eat once the bigger birds have gone.

I think of myself and wonder, am I persistent in my faith? Do I keep reading God's Word, delving deeper into what it says, getting kernels of truth that can blossom or nourish my soul?

Proverbs 3:3-4 says, "Let love and faithfulness never leave you; bind them around your neck, write them on the tablet of your heart. Then you will win favor and a good name in the sight of God and man." James 1:12 reminds me that "Blessed is the one who perseveres under trial because, having stood the test, that person will receive the crown of life that the Lord has promised to those who love him."

Prayer: Dear God, grant me the strength to persevere when times are tough; the faith to grow like a mustard seed as I seek to follow you. Thank you for walking with me all the days of my life so that I may dwell in the house of the Lord forever, Amen.

Taking Advantage of Time

It's an in-between-snow-flurries kind of morning and the black-capped chickadees are taking advantage of the chance to eat unimpeded by others at the bird feeder. They flit in and out, grabbing seeds as light snow floats downward. It's a cold morning too. Winter weather has returned, and the birds are hungry.

Since I needed to get to bed early so I could accompany my husband to his early doctor's appointment this morning, when I return I watch television shows recorded the night before. I start to doze.

By the time I wake, it is early afternoon, time to get busy. I need my second cup of coffee too. As I've said before, I'm not an early morning person.

The tufted titmice, the cardinals, the red-bellied woodpecker and some mourning doves join the black-capped chickadees. I see it's business as usual at the bird feeder.

I have a busy late afternoon and evening ahead of me. As I sip my brew, my husband comes into the room and laughs at my just getting used to the day at 1:40 pm. "I was glad you went with me this morning, but I see that when you get up early, your schedule gets all out of whack." He shakes his head as he looks at me rubbing my eyes and stifling a yawn.

He's right. But just like those birds, I love to take advantage of the time I usually have in the morning to go slowly into my day, eating breakfast, listening to my Bible app, reading God's Word and watching the birds. It's one great perk of retirement.

Ephesians 5:15 starts by cautioning me to be careful how I live, making the most of the opportunities God gives me. The King James version calls it 'redeeming the time' when I use my time wisely. Colossians 4:5 (NIV) says, "Be wise in the way you act toward outsiders; make the most of every opportunity." Titus 3:8 encourages and admonishes me to be careful to devote myself to doing what is good. As I take advantage of the opportunities to read God's Word, I may, as it says in Proverbs 2:1-15, gain wisdom and discretion that will protect me and guard me. It is God's wisdom that will save me from the ways of wicked people.

Prayer: Dear God, thank you for time to take advantage and read your Word, to gain your wisdom and learn discretion that will guide my path and protect me all the days of my life. Thank you, Amen.

Figure 12: Winter wonderland

Hidden Treasure

I watch two black-capped chickadees peck at the cold, hard, winter ground near the bird feeder. There's more food out farther, I want to tell them. It's all around in places you might not see at first, hidden treasures.

As is my habit, I empty the bottom of the bird feeder far away from the pole, scattering a good bit of seeds that are left when I bring it in to refill. This will help the mourning doves, since they need food too.

That makes me think of how often I forget or ignore God's goodness, his provisions, when I'm too busy to just sit and be still, listening to the Holy Spirit speak—like just now as I watch the two black-capped chickadees. How often do I overlook those chances to capture moments of wonder, food for the soul, as a teacher once told me. The hidden treasures, like God's Word, may come unbidden to view or my mind when I least expect it.

So, I need to store up God's Word, those memories, and hidden treasures just like it tells me in the Bible. Isaiah 45:3 says, "I will give you hidden treasures, riches stored in secret places, so that you may know I am the Lord, the God of Israel, who summons you by name." Psalm 119:11 reminds me to hide God's Word in my heart so that I do not sin against God. At the same time, I can recall these verses to restore, refresh, and protect me whenever I need it.

Prayer: Dear God, thank you for those moments, those memories and your Word that are hidden treasures that I may draw upon when I need you. Thank you for nature that draws me close to you, and thank you for my family, my friends, and the many blessings, you have given me. In Jesus' name I pray, Amen.

GOD'S PROVISION

Joy

I put my bird feeder out late this autumnal morning. As I drink my coffee and wait to see what birds will come, I tell myself it would be nice to see a cardinal, since I haven't seen them for a while. Suddenly two cardinals, a male and female, appear. What joy fills my heart to see these birds again.

Joy for a little bird: a great reminder of how God delights in us.

Then I realize this must be a shadow of what God feels when a long-lost person comes back to Him.

In Nehemiah 8:10, I am told that the joy of the Lord is our strength.

John 16:22 is a reminder that no one can take true joy from us. Even as I face and walk through hard and sometimes tragic times, God is walking with me. Isaiah 12:6 declares, "Shout aloud and sing for joy, people of Zion, for great is the Holy One of Israel among you."

I am encouraged to embrace God, and to greet Him every morning whether at a bird feeder, or as I drive to work. It is the meeting with God that gives me joy. He helps me face whatever lies ahead for the day. Deuteronomy 31:6 exhorts me to, "Be strong and courageous. Do not be afraid or terrified because of them, for the Lord your God goes with you; he will never leave you nor forsake you." Remember, God is with you. He delights in you. Find joy as you meet Him.

Prayer: God, help me to make time to greet you each morning, knowing you find joy in me. Please walk with me and guide me. Help me to find joy in the small things, knowing you are Lord of all. In Jesus' name I pray, Amen.

Movement

I sit at the table and watch a house finch scuttle around, eating seeds on the ground. Next, black-capped chickadees loop their way to the bird feeder. Tufted titmice and the white-breasted nuthatches swoop directly to the tall column-like tube holding the birdseed. Cardinals and mourning doves fly down to the ground, a pit stop for the red birds before they dart up to the feeder. The mourning doves contentedly peck at the seeds peeking out of the snow below.

The birds' methods of maneuvering remind me of how I move about in my life. Sometimes my goals are straightforward. I aim directly for them and achieve them—like the tufted titmice and white-breasted nuthatch. Other times I find myself looping ahead with ups and downs in my life as I strive for my goals—just like the black-capped chickadees.

Sometimes I am content to stay at the bottom, like the mourning doves—seeking sustenance where I am. Other times I soar and flit, seeking more elusive, higher goals.

What is important to remember is that like the varied flights of the birds, my path may change as I go through life. No matter what, however, I must remember God is with me as I swoop, loop, soar and rest. When I face detours, my path may look like the loops of the black-capped chickadees. God has His reasons for the detours. Sometimes it is to strengthen me for what lies ahead and other times it is to teach me something. In Exodus 13:17-18 I am told, "When Pharaoh let the people go, God did not lead them on the road through the Philistine country, though that was shorter. For God said, 'If they face war, they might change their minds and return to Egypt.'" So God led the people around the desert road toward the Red Sea.

God also directs and shows me the way He wants me to go as in Exodus 13:21: "By day the Lord went ahead of them in a pillar of cloud to guide them on their way and by night in a pillar of fire to give them light, so that they could travel by day or night."

Prayer: God, help me to fly like the birds, knowing you are there with me in the loops, in the soaring, and in the low places. Guide my thoughts to learn what you would have me learn as I go through my day. In Jesus' name I pray, Amen.

His Provisions

There are some snowy days that are so beautiful they take your breath away, so that only lyrical poetry can express what you see and what you think of God. Today was such a day for me.

Snow—
    Whipped by wind,
    Fondant icing on the ground.
Faces—
    On fence posts,
    Looking out and all around.
Chimes—
    Melodies,
    Swinging on breezes, go.
Plants—
    Deep in shrouds,
    Mounded shelter high and low.
Food—
    Swings in wind,
    The birds' beckoning signpost.
Gifts—
    God provides,
    What is needed by the most.

Figure 13: Provisions at the bird feeder

Prayer: Dear God, thank you for your provisions, tangible and intangible, for me as I look to you. Help me to rest in the knowledge that you care and will take care of me. In Jesus' name I pray, Amen.

What Do Birds and Animals Know That I Don't

As I stare out the window, I watch three mourning doves waddle under the birdfeeder. They usually graze on whatever seeds have dropped to the ground. Then a trio of black-capped chickadees flit around the feeder. I also see a squirrel running in the grass along the side of our yard. I haven't seen one since spring.

When I start to eat my breakfast, however, my attention is caught by a sight beyond my yard on the other side of our wire fence. A *huge* groundhog digs and pulls at grass and wood. Eventually it manages to carry something in its mouth into the wooded park behind our house. I have no idea what it is. Then I notice an increase in the number of birds and animals scurrying to get food.

It's early September, way too soon to start thinking about fall and winter. Then I wonder what these birds and animals know that I don't. My husband says it is instinct. I always question if it is more than that. Is God nudging these creatures to prepare for an early or harsh winter? Is the weather about to change? I think of the Scripture that says how God cares for the birds of the air. In Luke 12: 24 I am reminded how valuable I am. "Consider the ravens: They do not sow or reap, they have no storeroom or barn; yet God feeds them. And how much more valuable you are than birds!"

So, next time I start to wonder why the birds and animals seems to be eating more, I'll just remind myself this is God's way of taking care of them. Then when I worry or get concerned about the cares in my own life I'll note, if God takes care of these creatures, He will surely take care of me.

Prayer: God, help me to remember that you are in charge of all things, from the birds in the air and animals around us, to me and my cares and needs. Watch over us all, in Jesus' name. Thank you, Amen.

Taking Turns

It promises to be a warm sunny day today, so I refill my bird feeder then go inside to watch as the birds zero in on the fresh batch of seeds. The black-capped chickadees loop in first, then the tufted titmice, next the white-breasted nuthatch, and finally, the group of yellow finches. It is fascinating to watch them swoop down when there is an opening at the bird feeder. At times, birds line up on the metal hook above and alongside the feeder, waiting their turn. At other times, they become impatient, especially when the yellow finches perch on the various rungs of the feeder and above. Then others swoop in to challenge their dominance.

I am just like the birds waiting their turns. Sometimes I line up patiently, and other times I burst in, vying for attention. I've always heard that patience is a virtue, so I decide to examine Scripture that discusses patience.

Proverbs 15:8 tells me that hot tempers cause arguments, but patience brings peace.

Ecclesiastes 7:8 reminds me that patience is better than pride.

Hmm, so when I am impatient, I am prideful, putting myself, my concerns, and thoughts ahead of others. I cringe. That is something I need to work on. Looking further, I Corinthians 13:4 tells me: "Love is patient and kind. It does not envy, it does not boast, it is not proud." Feeling convicted, I can only stop and pray.

Prayer: Dear God, thank you that you are patient and merciful to me. Thank you for the birds, reminders of what I am, and how I should also strive to be. Please forgive me for my pride and arrogance. Continue to walk with me and guide me. Open the eyes of my heart to be more like you. In Jesus' name I pray, Amen.

En Garde

This morning a female red-winged blackbird grazes below the bird feeder. After every peck, the bird raises her head and looks around. The smaller birds give her a wide berth, perching elsewhere but not on the ground. Suddenly I hear some screeching. The red-winged blackbird hops into the bushes. A large shadow swoops down to the left of my window, chasing a smaller form. The red-winged blackbird and all the other birds disappear.

Is it one of the red-tailed hawks I have seen in the nearby woods? I'm not sure. I wait for a while, but the bird feeder and area around it remain deserted. The birds are very cautious. The Bible, in 1 Peter 5: 8 warns that Satan prowls like a lion, looking to see who he can devour.

That is why I am cautioned to be alert and to stand firm in my faith. 1 Peter 5:10 concludes by advising me that, then, after a little while, God will restore me and make me strong, firm, and steadfast.

So let me be like the red-winged blackbird, on guard, firm in my faith to endure trials and temptations.

Prayer: Dear God, thank you that you stand firm and are steadfast in your love for me. Guide me that I may be on guard for the darts and pain Satan throws my way, so that I may stand firm in my faith, knowing you will restore and heal me. In Jesus' name I pray, Amen.

Christmas Day Face-Off

It's day two of howling winds and frigid temperatures. In fact, it's Christmas Day here in Pittsburgh, PA. A day of giving as we share our joy in the greatest gift of all: JESUS. Outside birds are feasting on fallen seeds and those still in the feeder. I left it out overnight (my gift to the birds) and expect it to be empty this morning. It isn't. Instead, I see a myriad of birds jousting for the seeds on the ground and in the feeder. Along with juncos, song sparrows, and black-capped chickadees, there are tufted titmice and cardinals. Later a red-bellied woodpecker visits for a holiday meal.

I'm not sure if it is the temperature or the wind, but the birds seem feisty to me. I know they need to eat more for fuel when it's cold outside, but what I see is amazing. Usually, smaller birds give way to larger ones around the feeder. Not today.

As I eat my own breakfast, fuel for my start to the day, I see a song sparrow face off with a female cardinal. Later, another song sparrow (or maybe the same one) goes head-to-head with a male cardinal. Not to be outdone, a few moments later two male cardinals face off, this time in the air. I wish I could have captured that moment with my camera as they vie for territory and access to food.

It reminds me of how we as people fight for territory, for food, for survival. Right now, the birds need food to survive the howling winds and frigid temperatures. I wonder what our excuse is. The Bible says there will be wars and rumors of wars before Christ returns. With fighting in various regions of the world, the threat of war looms around us. Gazing outside, I renew my prayer for God to surround us with His peace and love.

Prayer: Dear God, may I know you walk with me through the howling winds of war and want. May I walk secure, knowing I can face the future with you by my side. Amen.

Figure 14: Christmas day face-off

Staying Under the Radar

I sip my coffee, enjoying the view out my window when I see them. There are two red-headed finches and a female cardinal eating at my bird feeder. Then the bigger birds come: a rose-breasted grosbeak and a red-bellied woodpecker. The finches and cardinal move away, but not very far. The grosbeak pokes its beak at the woodpecker, and it flies away, leaving the red-breasted grosbeak sole custody of the food.

Or so it thinks. A red-headed finch darts in the opposite direction of the bigger bird, managing to stay under the grosbeak's radar. The bigger bird keeps glancing to the left and right of its perch but the red-headed finch stays safe.

How many times in life have I gone under the radar, so to speak? As a little girl and now as an adult there are times I try to do things so people don't notice, not to get caught taking another cookie or doing something else I shouldn't. At other times, I watch others pursuing tasks they shouldn't, also seeming to go below the radar of getting noticed or caught.

But God sees all, unlike the red-breasted grosbeak. And God cares. He sees me and all I do, say, or think. In Psalm 139:1–4, David says, "You have searched me, Lord, and you know me. You know when I sit and when I rise; you perceive my thoughts from afar. You discern my going out and my lying down; you are familiar with all my ways. Before a word is on my tongue you, Lord, know it completely." I thank God for His loving watch over me.

Prayer: Dear God, bear with me when I try to fly below the radar, and bring me back into your will. Guide my ways so I follow your path and your desires for my life. In Jesus' name I pray, Amen.

Figure 15: Staying under the radar

Keeping Watch

This morning my stomach churns with anxiety (although I don't know why), and I seek solace in watching the birds. First a red cardinal stands guard on a post watching a female cardinal peck at seeds in the bird feeder. Then he goes to the ground and searches for seeds. A tiny red-headed finch perches on a middle rung, dipping its beak in the opening of the bird feeder. All seems well in the bird world. Even the two chipmunks frolic without a care in the tufts of tall grass that have sprung up after our recent late summer rain.

I take a deep breath and relax, thinking how great it is to have a place to unwind and shed my cares and worries. I'm reminded of Scripture that says not to worry because God is with us and cares, even as He cares for the birds of the air.

As I fight the tiny tendrils of worry that try to climb into my heart and mind, I claim Philippians 4:6: "Do not be anxious about anything, but in every situation, by prayer and petition, with thanksgiving, present your requests to God." In this unsettled world, I think about how God reminds me in Proverbs 3:5-7 to trust in Him, not depending on my own understanding of what is going on around me, but to give my cares and concerns to Him and He will untangle the confusion that threatens me. If I listen, He will direct me.

A big sigh wells up within me and I smile. Another male cardinal has come and is guarding the full bird feeder, perhaps for its companion, just like God guards my ways and watches over me.

Prayer: Dear God, thank you for restful places, for time to come to you and lay my burdens for family, for friends and for myself, in your hands. Thank you that I can crawl into your loving lap and surrender all. Thank you for your presence, for your healing touch when I am anxious. Thank you for your guidance at this very moment and in the moments to come. In Jesus' name I pray, Amen.

Sustenance

Once again, the birds have eaten all the seeds, scattering much of it on the ground. It's still cold outside and the ground is snow covered, so they need sustenance. So do I. As I sit in my warm room watching the birds peck and flit in the snow, I'm thankful for God's provisions for me and I pray for those less fortunate.

I remember when I needed help to get enough food for my family. My husband and I were both working, but after paying bills, the amount of money we had left didn't cover the cost of our food. I pecked and flitted in my own way to find generic food and supplies so I could keep costs down.

Looking out at the birds as they continue to search for food, I think I'll probably fill at least one of the bird feeders. It's the least I can do.

I'm reminded of Psalm 37:3-6 that tells us: "Trust in the Lord and do good; dwell in the land and enjoy safe pasture. Take delight in the Lord and he will give you the desires of your heart. Commit your way to the Lord; trust in him and he will do this: He will make your righteous reward shine like the dawn, your vindication like the noonday sun."

So, before I get my coat and boots on to go out to fill one of the bird feeders, I pray:

Dear God, thank you for your provisions for me. When I remember how my life was years ago and how you provided for me then, I am grateful. Thank you for your Word, your sustenance for my soul, and thank you for the birds, a reminder that you can use me as an instrument to care for others, even when they are only birds. In Jesus' name I pray, Amen.

Figure 16: Feeding time

Feasting

I put the filled bird feeder out late, past the time experts say birds usually dine. It's still out there three hours later and the birds are still visiting, grasping seeds at the four openings. It's a drizzly day, the snow has melted, leaving puddles for raindrops to splatter upon. The temperature has risen to a balmy (for Pittsburgh, PA in late winter) 52 degrees. So why are the birds still eating? I have no clue.

The expression "make hay while the sun shines," or in this case, eat while the bird seed is there, comes to mind. Feast, for the birds have no clue when it might be gone.

I wonder if we as humans realize the importance of feasting on God's Word. I have no idea what my future holds, but shouldn't I store up God's wisdom for whatever lies ahead?

Mark 13:31 tells me, "Heaven and earth will pass away, but my words will never pass away." John 6:63 says, "The Spirit gives life; the flesh counts for nothing. The words I have spoken to you they are full of the Spirit and life."

Not only does God's Word instruct, but it also uplifts, heals, and protects. Revelation speaks of the end time when Christ shall come again. Rev. 19:11-13 says, "I saw heaven standing open and there before me was a white horse, whose rider is called Faithful and True. With justice he judges and wages war. His eyes are like blazing fire, and on his head are many crowns. He has a name written on him that no one knows but he himself. He is dressed in a robe dipped in blood, and his name is the Word of God."

Prayer: Dear God, I don't know the future. Help me to learn your Word so that I may be sustained, just like the birds at the feeder, seeking their fill. Restore my soul. I pray I may dwell in your presence now and forever more. Amen.

Red-tailed Hawk Attack

I am at my table as a tufted titmouse and a black-capped chickadee eat seeds outside. All is peaceful. Out of the corner of my eye I see a large shadow swoop into view. I look up in time to spy a red-tailed hawk dive at the birds. I can't tell if the hawk captures one of them or not. Then a second hawk appears, following it. They swoop to a tree fifty yards away. There is some flitting around, then the second hawk takes off. As I watch, white feathers float down from where the hawk perches with its prey. It has something.

Poor little bird. Is it the black-capped chickadee or the tufted titmouse? I'm not sure I really want to know. It never stood a chance. The attack is so sudden. As the hawk sits on the long limb, pecking away at whatever is caught in its claws, other tufted titmice and black-capped chickadees fly to the bird feeder, snatch seeds and fly to safety.

The sudden attack on the smaller birds reminds me of how Satan loves to swoop into our lives taking our joy… and our peace. In turbulent times I like to think of myself as being able to climb up onto God's lap to let His love and peace surround me. Galatians 4:6a and Romans 8:15 both say, "The Spirit you received does not make you slaves, so that you live in fear again; rather the Spirit you received brought about your adoption to sonship [in my case, to daughtership]. And by him we cry, 'Abba, Father'."

So, I know that whenever Satan tries to move in and steal my peace, like the red-tailed hawk grabbed the bird, I can call out to my Heavenly Father to come and surround me with His love and strength. He is truly my Abba, Father.

Prayer: Dear God, please help me keep my eyes on you when trouble assails me. Thank you for your son, Jesus, and the Holy Spirit to guide me. Amen.

Recharging

I need to recharge the camera battery on the bird feeder on my deck. That'll take at least twenty-four hours. I go outside to empty the few seeds left in the other bird feeder on the ground before I bring it in to the house to refill. I'm debating filling it before I finish writing this observation.

Sigh, I guess I should do it before it rains. Then again, I did dump a lot of seeds on the ground. Ah, the persistent black-capped chickadees have found those seeds on the ground. The mourning doves will soon be there too.

Okay, I fill and take out the bird feeder. The tufted titmouse is eating. We'll see if any other birds eat this late in the morning. I'm not going to fill the other bird feeder until the battery has recharged and is put back into it.

Talking or writing about recharging reminds me how important it is for all God's creatures to recharge our own batteries. I do it by eating and sleeping. I also know that I need to recharge my soul. I do this in a variety of ways: meditating, doing something creative, a physical activity or singing, playing a musical instrument, or painting a picture.

I find that when I spend quiet time watching the birds (the black-capped chickadees and the cardinals are back) it helps refresh my soul and my mind.

Prayer: Dear God, thank you for family, friends, nature, and time to spend however I need, to recharge my battery. Thank you for your Word, the Holy Spirit, and Jesus. Amen.

The Uncertain Lull

There's a lull at the bird feeder. I relax in the quiet, but only for a moment. Oops, a blue jay has noticed the full feeder. Its raucous call alerts other birds. Here come more black-capped chickadees, the male and female cardinals, and the tufted titmice, all ready to eat the seeds.

How often do you have a lull in your life when you can just be still? I know when I was a young mother, it was rare. I see the same thing with my son and his wife who have two young boys. It's hard to find time to rest and recharge. They, like me, need to take advantage of any lulls in life to rest and just be still. One of my favorite Bible verses when I was younger and still today, is Matthew 11:28 that says, "Come to me, all you who are weary and burdened, and I will give you rest." I used to picture myself climbing up into God's lap to get that rest.

As an older adult, I have and cherish times of rest. 1 Kings 5:4 talks about how the Israelites had rest on every side. In Job, God tells Job to have hope because God will protect him and allow him to rest safely. Psalm 3:5 and Psalm 4:8 says that the Lord sustains me, I can sleep and wake, trusting Him. Psalm 23 reminds me that God restores my soul. With these reassurances I know I can rest easy.

Prayer: Dear God, help me to remember to claim the promises in your Word to restore my soul, that I may rest in the lulls of life and in the busyness as well, knowing you are my safety and shield. Amen.

Red-Headed Finches and Mourning Doves

It always amazes me when I see the variety of birds that come to eat at the feeder. Watching the red-headed finches feast on seeds while the mourning doves pick up kernels of food on the ground makes me smile. The variety in nature is astounding. Just like the variety in the human race.

God has made all of us and glories in our differences. I need to remember that in my daily interaction with others. Kindness to strangers is important; just like Jesus tells us, I need to love my neighbor as myself. Jesus continues with this admonition when he recounts that parable of the Good Samaritan who helps an injured man in Luke 10: 25-37. The Samaritan goes above and beyond what might be expected of him.

As I look at the two red-headed finches I can see one is the male and the other is the female. They come together to eat and watch out for each other. The male and female cardinal usually come at the same time too. They are all so different, yet they come together to help each other when they eat.

God's variety, like those found in nature, shows His creativity and His delight in all creatures. I should remember that and take delight in just accepting the differences I perceive in others.

Prayer: Dear God, thank you that your love is so great and so deep and so wide that you have created such diversity on earth. Help me to be kind and to care for those not like me. Help me to delight in your creation all around me. Amen.

GLOSSARY OF BIRDS

Black-capped chickadees live in and near forests. They are inquisitive, plucky, hide seeds and other food items to eat later (in over 1000 different places), and every autumn these birds allow brain neurons containing old information to die, replacing them with new neurons so they can adapt to changes in their social flocks and environment even with their tiny brains.

Blue jays live in trees in forests. They are intelligent and inquisitive and will often dominate a bird feeder until a woodpecker comes along. They are very vocal and like to sing when perched high in a tree. They can mimic the call of the red-tailed hawk, and love to gather food and bury it for later use. They are credited for helping to expand the number of oak trees in North America.

Cardinals live in woodlands, gardens, shrubs, trees, and wetlands. They usually come to the feeder in pairs as in this picture. They are very nurturing of their young and may have up to 3 clutches of eggs. They feed their young seeds and insects and can be seen to put food directly into the mouths of their fledglings. The baby cardinal is pale brown and gray mostly.

Cowbirds live in open fields, pastures, meadows, and forest edges. They are large black-bodied birds with dull brown heads. They are called brood parasites because they lay their eggs in other birds' nests and let other birds raise their young. If the host bird destroys their egg, the cowbirds will retaliate and destroy the host birds' eggs and nest.

Downy woodpeckers are the smallest of the North American woodpeckers and can be found in forests of the United States and Canada. They are just 6 to 7 inches long and build their nest in tree cavities, feeding on insects and seeds and berries. The male usually creates the nest in the deadwood of a tree and the female will lay 4-7 white eggs. During the day, both birds take turns incubating the eggs in 15-minute shifts. At night the male rests on the eggs for their continued warmth. Eggs hatch after twelve days.

Finches —Red-headed finches and gold finches live in wooded areas. They visit the bird feeder with their mates. The vivid colors of the male are acquired from their diet and are used to attract female mates. Red plumage tends to attract first-year females who then must work hard to feed the chicks since the red-headed males don't. On the other hand, an orange or yellow-headed male finch will help feed chicks, thus making them more attractive to older female finches.

Grackles nest in dense trees, pines, or shrubs, near water. They are large black birds with iridescent wings and a body with a large beak. A group of grackles is called a plague. They love to eat a variety of grains.

Juncos live in woodlands and forests, migrating south in the winter. They are small, black-bodied birds with a white underside and are part of the sparrow family.

Mourning doves live in grasslands, prairies, farms, and urban areas. They have been known by many names, including the rain dove, chueybird, and the turtle dove. The further north they live, the further south they may migrate. When nest building, the male gathers supplies and the female builds the nest. The bird is a strong flier, capable of speeds up to 55 mph. They are monogamous, with two squabs (young) per brood. Both parents care for the young, feeding them crop milk.

Red-bellied woodpeckers lives in deciduous forests and nest in decayed cavities of dead trees, old stumps or in live trees that have softer wood such as elms, maples, or willows. It is a medium-sized woodpecker with a vivid red-orange crown and reddish blush on its lower underside. They are omnivores, eating insects, fruits, nuts, and seeds. The birds are monogamous, the males locating a nest hole and seeking the mate's approval by mutual tapping. If she approves, the female completes the excavation and enters the nest hole. They are territorial during the nesting season which begins in April or May and stay in that area for a year or more.

Red-winged blackbirds live along watercourses, wet roadsides, as well as drier meadows and old fields. Males are glossy black with red and yellow shoulder badges. Females are crisply streaked and dark brownish in color, paler on the breast and may show a whitish eyebrow. Males like to sit on high perches and sing, while the female stays lower, skulking though vegetation for food and quietly weaving together their nests. They gather in larger groups in winter to eat grains.

Red-tailed hawks are birds of prey that usually hunt with their partner. They can acclimate to all biomes within their range, occurring on the edges of open woodlands. They like to eat rodents, small birds, and other animals.

Robins live in woodlands, farmlands, and hedgerows where they eat insects and worms. Here we see a baby robin that is foraging for food in the grass. Robins in turn are eaten by foxes, bobcats, hawks, and shrikes, while owls, crows, and blue jays often take their eggs and babies. These friendly songbirds are comfortable around people.

Rose-breasted grosbeaks live in temperate, open, deciduous woods. They are part of the Cardinal family and are large seed-eating birds. Pictured here is a female grosbeak on the left and the more colorful rose-breasted male grosbeak on the right. Their maximum lifespan in the wild is about 7 years.

 Song sparrows are seed eating songbirds in North America who nest in backyards, fields, bushy areas near water, and marshes, tucking their deep cup (nest) of grasses right on the ground or in flowerbeds or bushes. While song sparrows are one of the most numerous birds on earth, their number has declined in recent years due to pesticides and loss of nesting places. They live on average 11 years.

Tufted titmice live in deciduous and mixed woods and are small songbirds in the Tit and Chickadee family. Males are larger than females and recognizable for their white front, and gray upper body with rust-colored flanks. They also have a tufted gray crest on their heads. While they are seed and berry eaters, they will also eat insects and in the summer favor caterpillars as a major part of their diet. These birds form small flocks known as troupes or bandrites which often include chickadees when foraging. Their lifespan is about 2 years although they can live for more than 10 years. Many offspring of tufted titmice will stay with their parents during the first winer and after the first year of their life.

White-breasted nuthatches live in mature woods and woodlands. They have long beaks, large heads, almost no neck, and a short tail. These birds are agile, creeping along tree trunks and large branches, probing into holes and cracks. They often turn sideways and upside down on vertical surfaces. They eat mostly insects and seeds. Their predators are hawks and owls. Squirrels and snakes may eat their nestlings and eggs.

Other Creatures

Chipmunks live in deciduous forests, forest edges, brush, meadows, and gardens. They are small, striped rodents in the squirrel family. They typically live 3 years and can be 8-10 inches long. They get their name from the "chip, chip" sound they make. The male, called a "buck," mates with the female, called a "doe," twice a year, in the spring and late summer. The female chipmunk raises the "pups" but is not close to the chipmunks once they leave.

Groundhogs live in lowlands of North America. They are also called woodchucks and are part of the rodent family belonging to the group of large ground squirrels known as marmots. A few of the more picturesque nicknames they are known by are "whistle pig," "whistler," "groundpig," and "land beaver." The Lenape called them "Monax" which means "digger." The groundhog is thought to be a very important habitat engineer. They live in aggregations and are the least social of the marmot species. The males and females do not form long-term bonds with each other. They are considered extremely intelligent animals, with complex social networks, able to understand social behavior and form kinship with their young, communicate through whistling, and work cooperatively to solve tasks such as burrowing. They can climb trees to escape predators. In the wild they live an average of 2-3 years.

Photographs in this glossary are the author's except for the red-tailed hawk which was a stock photo in Microsoft Office, and the junco from DepositPhotos. You can find more information about the birds from various internet sites such as: the Audubon Society, Cornell Lab of Ornithology and Wikipedia as well as https://www.allaboutbirds.com.

ABOUT THE AUTHOR

JANET LYNN PIERCE, PhD, is a retired English as a Second Language teacher, former newspaper reporter, and feature writer for the *Pittsburgh Tribune Review* and editor, reporter, and photographer for the weekly *Community News Standard Observer*. She has written historical nonfiction articles for newspapers, informational articles for Pennwriters, St. Davids' Christian Writers, and TESOL International, and newsletters for professional organizations. Recent publications include poems, flash fiction, and a creative nonfiction story. She is available for workshops and presentations.

Blog: www.janetpierceswritingcafe.com

Facebook: www.facebook.com/janetpierceauthor

Instagram: @jpierce494

www.ingramcontent.com/pod-product-compliance
Lightning Source LLC
Chambersburg PA
CBHW041240020426

42333CB00002B/25